How To

Utilize Your

Full Potential

A Practical Guide

By: Frank Sumera

The little book that's loaded with a lot of useful information.

In Loving Memory of

Frana Spanja

1921-2014

"I'm finally doing it Baba!"

i

Acknowledgements

I'd like to thank George Doran, Arthur Miller and James Cunningham for
coining their S.M.A.R.T goals that have made a contribution into this book
and had a significant impact to me when
I was thinking of how to write.
Cheers Gentleman

Contents

Acknowledgements i

Introduction

Are you looking to unlock your full potential and achieve your goals? In "How To Utilize Your Full Potential," you will learn practical strategies and tools for harnessing your inner talents and abilities.

This book offers a step-by-step approach to identifying your strengths, setting clear goals, developing a growth mindset, understanding and developing emotional intelligence , seeking feedback, and taking risks. You'll discover how to overcome obstacles and push past your limitations to achieve success in your personal and professional life.

With insights from psychology, neuroscience, and personal development strategies this book offers a comprehensive guide to unlocking your potential. You'll learn how to shift your mindset from fixed to growth, cultivate self-awareness, and develop a personalized plan for achieving your goals.

Whether you're a student, professional, or simply looking to achieve personal growth, "How To Utilize Your Full Potential " provides practical advice and inspiration for unlocking your full potential. With actionable strategies, this book will empower you to live a more fulfilling and successful life.

Chapter -2
Psychological
Self-Neglect

This chapter is classified as -2 due to being in the state of a negative mental deficit with one's self and in one's own mind. Playing the role of a victim of everything that has gone wrong.

Psychological self-neglect is a form of self-sabotage that can lead to significant emotional, mental, and even physical health problems. It occurs when individuals fail to take care of their own mental needs, resulting in feelings of hopelessness, despair, and disconnection from themselves and others.

This can lead to a range of negative consequences, including decreased quality of life, poor physical health, and increased risk of mental health disorders such as depression, anxiety, and substance abuse.

Psychological self-neglect can manifest in various ways, such as neglecting one's own needs for rest and relaxation, avoiding seeking help for emotional or mental health problems, failing to establish and maintain healthy relationships, and engaging in self-destructive behaviors such as substance abuse, disordered eating, or even risky sexual behaviors.

How To Utilize Your Full Potential

Here are some strategies that can help individuals to deal with psychological self-neglect:

1.Recognize the Problem

The first step in dealing with psychological self-neglect is recognizing that there is a problem. This can involve taking an honest inventory of one's mental health and emotional well-being, and acknowledging any areas of concern. This may involve recognizing negative patterns of thinking or behavior that are contributing to the problem.

2.Seek Support

Support can come from a variety of sources, such as friends, family, and mental health professionals. It is important to seek support from those who can offer emotional support, guidance, and encouragement. Seeking support can help individuals feel less alone, and provide a sense of community that can help to counteract feelings of self-neglect.

3.Practice Self-Compassion

Self-compassion involves treating oneself with kindness and understanding, and avoiding self-criticism or judgment. It is essential for individuals who are dealing with psychological self-neglect, as it can help to counteract feelings of shame or self-blame. By practicing self-compassion, individuals can develop a sense of acceptance and resilience that can help them to overcome the negative effects of self-neglect.

4.Develop Healthy Habits

Developing healthy habits is key to overcoming psychological self-neglect. This can involve establishing a routine that includes time for self-care, such as exercise, meditation, or relaxation techniques. It may also involve developing healthy habits around food and sleep, and taking care to prioritize these needs. Developing healthy habits can help individuals to feel more in control of their lives, and provide a sense of

structure that can help to counteract feelings of self-neglect.

5.Challenge Negative Thoughts

Negative thoughts can contribute to feelings of self-neglect by reinforcing self-doubt and a sense of hopelessness. To counteract these negative thoughts, it can be helpful to challenge them by examining the evidence for and against them. For example, if an individual is struggling with feelings of worthlessness, they may examine the evidence for and against this belief, and work to develop a more balanced and realistic perspective.

6.Address Underlying Issues

Psychological self-neglect can be rooted in underlying issues such as past inflicted trauma, low self-esteem, or mental health disorders. Addressing these underlying issues can be essential to overcoming self-neglect. This may involve seeking therapy or counseling, or working with a mental health professional to develop a treatment plan that addresses these underlying issues.

7.Practice Self-Reflection

Practicing self-reflection can help individuals to identify patterns of behavior or thought that contribute to self-neglect, and develop strategies to overcome them. This may involve journaling, meditation, or other techniques that allow individuals to reflect on their thoughts and emotions in a non-judgmental way.

How To Utilize Your Full Potential

In conclusion, psychological self-neglect is a pattern of behavior that can have serious consequences for mental health and well-being. However, by recognizing the problem, seeking support, practicing self-compassion, developing healthy habits, challenging negative thoughts, addressing underlying issues, and practicing self-reflection, individuals can overcome self-neglect

Chapter -1
Understanding
Emotional
Self-Neglect

Emotional self-neglect is a common but often overlooked phenomenon that can have a significant impact on one's well-being. It refers to the failure to take care of one's emotional needs, leading to a lack of self-awareness, self-care, and self-compassion.

Emotional self-neglect can manifest in a variety of ways, such as ignoring one's feelings, suppressing emotions, denying oneself pleasurable experiences, or neglecting relationships and social support systems. This essay will explore the causes, consequences, and strategies to overcome emotional self-neglect.

Causes of Emotional Self-Neglect

There are several factors that contribute to emotional self-neglect. Childhood experiences, such as growing up in an environment where emotions were not validated or were seen as a weakness, can make it difficult for an individual to acknowledge and express their feelings.

Additionally, societal and cultural expectations that emphasize productivity, achievement, and self-reliance can lead individuals to prioritize work over self-care or neglect their emotional needs.

Trauma, such as abuse, neglect, or loss, can also contribute to emotional self-neglect by making it difficult for individuals to trust others, feel safe expressing their emotions, or engage in self-care activities.

Consequences of Emotional Self-Neglect

Emotional self-neglect can have significant consequences on an individual's well-being. One of the most significant consequences is the development of mental health issues such as depression, anxiety, and stress. When an individual does not take care of their emotional needs, it can lead to a buildup of negative emotions and thoughts, which can manifest in various physical and emotional symptoms.

For example, prolonged stress and anxiety can cause physical symptoms such as headaches, muscle tension, and fatigue.

Emotional self-neglect can also impact an individual's relationships with others. Neglecting emotional needs can make it difficult to form and maintain meaningful connections with others. Individuals who engage in emotional self-neglect may struggle with intimacy, vulnerability, and trust, which can make it challenging to establish healthy relationships.

How To Utilize Your Full Potential

Strategies to Overcome Emotional Self-Neglect

Overcoming emotional self-neglect requires a willingness to prioritize emotional self-care and take steps to address unmet emotional needs. Here are some strategies that can help individuals overcome emotional self-neglect:

1.Develop Self-Awareness:
The first step in overcoming emotional self-neglect is developing self-awareness. This involves acknowledging and accepting one's emotions, thoughts, and behaviors without judgment. It can be helpful to keep a journal, practice mindfulness, or seek therapy to develop self-awareness.

2.Practice Self-Care:
Engaging in self-care activities is essential for emotional well-being. Self-care can include activities such as exercise, meditation, spending time in nature, pursuing hobbies, or seeking social support.

3.Set Boundaries:
 Setting boundaries is crucial in preventing emotional self-neglect. Boundaries can help individuals prioritize their emotional needs, reduce stress, and establish healthy relationships.

4.Seek Professional Help:
Individuals who struggle with emotional self-neglect may benefit from seeking professional help, such as therapy or counseling. A mental health professional can help individuals develop coping strategies, overcome negative patterns of thinking, and improve emotional well-being.

5.Practice Self-Compassion:

Finally, it's essential to practice self-compassion. Self-compassion involves treating oneself with kindness, understanding, and acceptance. It can be helpful to practice positive self-talk, challenge negative self-beliefs, and engage in self-care activities that promote self-compassion.

Conclusion

In conclusion, emotional self-neglect is a prevalent but often overlooked phenomenon that can have significant consequences on an individual's well-being. Childhood experiences, societal and cultural expectations, and trauma can all contribute to emotional self-neglect.

Chapter 0
Building
Resilience

This chapter is classified as ground zero for me. From rock bottom we have a place to plant our feet to ignite our inner phoenix that burns off all the impurities of failure and the fall just to rise again only stronger and wiser than ever before. The realization of resilience is the idea that whatever has happened to you may have hurt you mentally or even physically but it didn't diminish your life force, the spark within you to continue. Through my personal experiences it has given me the understanding to mentally regroup, reorganize and try again.

Resilience is the ability to adapt and cope with life's challenges and setbacks. It is a critical skill that allows individuals to bounce back from difficult situations, such as job loss, relationship problems, health issues, and more. Building resilience is an essential aspect of living to your full potential as it helps you navigate life's ups and downs with greater ease and grace.

In this chapter we will explore the importance of building resilience and provide practical strategies to help you develop this critical skill.

How To Utilize Your Full Potential

Why is Resilience Important?

Resilience is an important quality because it allows individuals to overcome adversity and continue moving forward towards their goals. It enables people to maintain a positive attitude, even in the face of setbacks and challenges, and to keep striving for success. Resilient individuals are better equipped to cope with stress, manage their emotions, and maintain healthy relationships.

Moreover, resilience is an essential aspect of mental health. Individuals with high levels of resilience are less likely to develop depression, anxiety, and other mental health disorders. They are better equipped to cope with the stress of everyday life and are more likely to maintain a positive outlook on life.

Strategies for Building Resilience

Building resilience is a process that requires consistent effort over time.

The following strategies can help you develop this critical skill:

1.Cultivate a Positive Attitude
A positive attitude is a key component of resilience. It helps individuals maintain a hopeful outlook, even in the face of adversity. To cultivate a positive attitude, focus on the good in your life, practice gratitude, and engage in positive self-talk. Instead of dwelling on your failures or shortcomings, focus on your strengths and accomplishments.

2.Develop Strong Relationships

Having strong relationships with friends, family, and other support networks is critical for building resilience. These relationships provide a sense of belonging and support that can help individuals cope with difficult situations. To build strong relationships, make an effort to connect with others, listen actively, and show empathy.

3.Practice Self-Care

Self-care is critical for maintaining resilience. It allows individuals to prioritize their physical and mental health, which in turn helps them cope with stress and adversity. To practice self-care, prioritize getting enough sleep, eating a healthy diet, and engaging in regular exercise. Additionally, engage in activities that bring you joy and help you relax, such as reading, taking a bath, or meditating.

4.Build Problem-Solving Skills

Effective problem-solving skills are an essential aspect of resilience. Individuals who are skilled at problem-solving are better equipped to handle difficult situations and find solutions to challenges.

To build problem-solving skills, focus on identifying the problem, brainstorming possible solutions, and implementing the best solution.

5.Practice Mindfulness

Mindfulness is the practice of being present and fully engaged in the current moment. It is a powerful tool for building resilience as it helps individuals stay focused on the present rather than dwelling on past failures or future worries. To practice mindfulness, focus on your breath, engage your senses, and cultivate a non-judgmental attitude towards your thoughts and feelings.

In conclusion, building resilience is critical for living to your full potential. It allows individuals to cope with stress and adversity, maintain a positive outlook, and keep moving forward towards their goals. By cultivating a positive attitude, developing strong relationships, practicing self-care, building problem-solving skills, and practicing mindfulness, you can develop the critical skill of resilience and live your best life. Remember that building resilience is a process that requires consistent effort over time, but the rewards are well worth the effort.

Overcoming adversity

Adversity is a part of life that can strike anyone at any time. It can come in many forms, such as illness, financial hardship, personal loss, death of a loved one or unexpected changes. Whatever the cause, adversity can be a difficult and painful experience that can leave us feeling overwhelmed and helpless. However, it is possible to recover from adversity and emerge stronger and more resilient than ever before.

The first step in recovering from adversity is to acknowledge and accept the situation. It is natural to feel angry, frustrated, or sad when faced with adversity, but denying or avoiding the situation will only prolong the pain. Instead, it is important to face the situation head-on and accept that it has happened.

The next step is to take action. This may involve seeking support from family and friends, seeking professional help, or taking steps to address the problem directly. For example, if the adversity is financial, it may involve creating a budget or seeking financial advice. If the adversity is a health issue, it may involve seeking medical treatment or making lifestyle changes.

How To Utilize Your Full Potential

One of the most important things to remember when recovering from adversity is to take care of yourself. This includes eating well, getting enough sleep, and engaging in activities that bring you joy and relaxation. Self-care is essential for maintaining physical and emotional well-being, and can help you to feel more resilient and better able to cope with adversity.

Another important factor in recovering from adversity is to maintain a positive outlook. This can be difficult when faced with difficult and challenging circumstances, but it is essential for staying motivated and focused on the future. A positive outlook can help you to see the opportunities that may arise from adversity, and can help you to stay hopeful and optimistic about the future.

It is also important to cultivate a sense of gratitude. This involves focusing on the things in your life that you are grateful for, even in the midst of adversity. Gratitude can help to shift your focus away from the challenges you are facing and towards the positive aspects of your life. It can also help you to feel more connected to others and to the world around you.

Another important factor in recovering from adversity is to stay connected to others. This may involve seeking support from family and friends, or joining a support group or community organization. Staying connected to others can help you to feel less isolated and alone, and can provide a source of encouragement and motivation.

Finally, it is important to be patient and persistent. Recovering from adversity is not a quick or easy process, and it may involve setbacks and challenges along the way. However, with patience and persistence, it is possible to overcome adversity and emerge stronger and more resilient than ever before.

How To Utilize Your Full Potential

In conclusion, recovering from adversity is a process that requires acceptance, action, self-care, a positive outlook, gratitude, connection, and persistence. By taking these steps, it is possible to overcome adversity and emerge stronger and more resilient than ever before. Remember, you are not alone in your struggles, and there is always hope for a better future.

Chapter 1
Living Up To
Your Potential

Living up to your potential is something that many people strive for, but few truly achieve. It's a vague concept that can be difficult to define, but essentially it means being the best version of yourself and making the most of your talents, skills, and abilities. It involves setting and achieving goals, pushing yourself out of your comfort zone, and constantly striving to improve. In this chapter, we will explore what it means to live up to your potential, the benefits of doing so, and the common barriers that prevent people from reaching their full potential.

Defining Potential

Potential is defined as the capacity to develop and become something more. It's the innate ability that we all possess to achieve great things and make a positive impact on the world around us. Potential is not just about talent or intelligence, it's also about attitude, work ethic, and perseverance. It's about having a growth mindset and believing that you can learn, grow, and improve over time.

How To Utilize Your Full Potential

Living Up to Your Potential

Living up to your potential means striving to be the best version of yourself. It's about setting high standards for yourself and working hard to achieve them. It's about pushing yourself out of your comfort zone and taking risks. It's about constantly learning, growing, and improving. It's about making the most of your talents, skills, and abilities and using them to make a positive impact on the world around you.

Benefits of Living Up to Your Potential

There are many benefits to living up to your potential. Here are a few of the most significant:

1.Personal Growth:
 Living up to your potential requires you to constantly learn, grow, and improve. This leads to personal growth and development, which can be incredibly rewarding.

2.Increased Confidence:
Achieving your goals and living up to your potential can boost your confidence and self-esteem. You'll feel more capable and empowered, which can have a positive impact on all areas of your life.

3.Fulfillment:
When you're living up to your potential, you're doing something meaningful and purposeful. This can bring a sense of fulfillment and satisfaction that is hard to find elsewhere.

How To Utilize Your Full Potential

4.Success:

Living up to your potential can lead to success in all areas of your life, whether it's in your career, relationships, or personal life. When you're striving to be the best version of yourself, you're more likely to achieve your goals and succeed.

Barriers to Living Up to Your Potential

Despite the many benefits of living up to your potential, there are many barriers that can prevent people from doing so. Here are a few of the most common:

1.Fear:

Fear is a powerful barrier that can prevent us from taking risks and stepping outside of our comfort zone. Fear of failure, fear of success, and fear of the unknown can all hold us back from living up to our potential.

2.Lack of Self-Confidence:

If you don't believe in yourself, it's hard to live up to your potential. A lack of self-confidence can lead to self-doubt and a fear of failure, which can prevent you from taking risks and pursuing your goals.

3.Procrastination:

Procrastination is a common barrier that can prevent us from achieving our goals. When we put things off, we delay our progress and miss out on opportunities to grow and improve.

4.Negative Self-Talk: The way we talk to ourselves can have a big impact on our ability to live up to our potential. Negative self-talk can lead to self-doubt and a lack of confidence, which can
prevent us from pursuing our goals.

5.Lack of Motivation:
If you're not motivated to achieve your goals, it's hard to live up to your potential. A lack of motivation can trigger a state of depression which can potentially lead you to a place of procrastination and a negative outlook on every area of your life.

It's important to understand that your potential is not fixed, but rather it is a dynamic and ever-evolving aspect of yourself. By cultivating a growth mindset and embracing challenges, you can continue to develop and expand your potential throughout your life.

It's also important to recognize that everyone's potential is unique, and there is no one-size-fits-all approach to unlocking your full potential. You may have different strengths and weaknesses than others, and your goals and aspirations may differ as well. That's why it's important to take the time to reflect on your own values, interests, and passions, and to set goals that align with these aspects of yourself.

Furthermore, your potential is not solely determined by your abilities and intelligence. External factors such as access to resources, opportunities, and support systems can also play a significant role in unlocking your full potential. That's why it's important to seek out mentors, coaches, and other support systems to help you navigate challenges and achieve your goals.

In summary, understanding your potential is about recognizing that it is dynamic and ever-evolving, and that cultivating a growth mindset and embracing challenges can help you continue to develop and expand your potential throughout your life. By setting goals that align with your values and passions, and seeking out support systems to help you navigate challenges, you can unlock your full potential and achieve your dreams.

This is the core understanding of why we live our lives, add meaning and understanding. The world is but a stage and we are playing the main role to our own ever evolving scenarios that build you into the role you are continually meant to become. You are the master of your destiny happening to the world by taking responsibility of it no matter what has happened to you in the past leading to this very moment of your life or you are the victim of your circumstances allowing everything that has happened to you affect you and have an overpowering impact on how you see yourself in this world.

You are a force, an energy that comes with its own bespoke needs and desires. Each and every one of us comes to this 3 dimensional space with our own special qualities of individuality that is living deeply within us. We do learn from every experience, be it negative or positive, but every experience adds wisdom and a potential to grow from it or reduce into self-doubt. We are on a journey of self realization, the power and the force is within us, it always was and always will be, but when our attention is always on everything else we fail to stay focused on what's within.

Imagine if we were taught this at the beginning as children when our minds were like sponges. Where would you be now? Everything is teaching us something new about ourselves. Our progression would move so much more quickly to a life we feel we deserve created from within and materializing outward. You would be a lot more careful at what you'd say to your soon to be you. If you already knew what's in store for you and it was pure joy and contentment you'd only be trying to live at the higher vibration of your full potential to get there.

FS

Chapter 2
Identifying Your
Strengths and Weaknesses

One of the key steps to living up to your potential is to identify your strengths and weaknesses. This can help you to focus your efforts on areas where you excel and identify areas where you need to improve.

In this chapter, we will explore why it's important to identify your strengths and weaknesses, how to do so, and how to use this information to achieve your goals.

Why Identify Your Strengths and Weaknesses?

Identifying your strengths and weaknesses is important for several
reasons:

1.Maximizing Your Potential:
By identifying your strengths, you can focus your efforts on areas where you excel and maximize your potential. You can also identify areas where you need to improve and work on developing those skills.

How To Utilize Your Full Potential

2.Personal Growth:

Understanding your weaknesses can be difficult, but it's an important step in personal growth. By acknowledging your weaknesses, you can take steps to address them and become a better version of yourself.

3.Career Advancement:

Identifying your strengths and weaknesses can also help you in your career. By focusing on areas where you excel, you can position yourself for advancement and success. By addressing your weaknesses, you can improve your performance and become a more valuable employee or a leader to your employees as they will see a more humanistic side of you.

How to Identify Your Strengths and Weaknesses

Identifying your strengths and weaknesses can be a challenging process, but there are several methods that can help:

1.Self-Reflection:

Take some time to reflect on your experiences and accomplishments. Think about the tasks or activities that come easily to you and the ones that you find more challenging. Consider the feedback that you've received from others and what you've learned from your successes and failures.

2.Feedback from Others:

Ask for feedback from people who know you well, such as friends, family, or colleagues.

How To Utilize Your Full Potential

Ask them to identify your strengths and weaknesses and be open to their feedback.

3.Personality Assessments:

Personality assessments, such as the Myers-Briggs Type Indicator or the StrengthsFinder assessment, can help you to identify your personality traits and strengths.

4.Skill Assessments:

There are many skill assessments available that can help you to identify your strengths and weaknesses in specific areas, such as communication, leadership, or problem-solving. A link that I have found helpful is :

https://www.thecareertest.org
There are many to choose from online.

Using Your Strengths and Weaknesses to Achieve Your Goals
Once you've identified your strengths and weaknesses, it's important to use this information to achieve your goals.

Here are some tips on how to do so:

1.Build on Your Strengths:

Use your strengths to your advantage. Focus on areas where you excel and look for opportunities to use these strengths to achieve your goals.

2.Address Your Weaknesses:

Don't ignore your weaknesses. Instead, take steps to address them. This may involve seeking training or education, practicing new skills, or seeking feedback and guidance from others.

3.Set Realistic Goals:

When setting goals, be realistic about your strengths and weaknesses. Set goals that are challenging, but also achievable given your current skill set and resources.

4.Seek Support:

Don't be afraid to seek support from others. Whether it's a mentor, coach, or friend, having someone to provide guidance and encouragement can be incredibly helpful in achieving your goals.

Examples of Using Your Strengths and Weaknesses to Achieve Your Goals

Here are some examples of how to use your strengths and weaknesses to achieve your goals:

1.Career Advancement:

If you're looking to advance in your career, identify your strengths and weaknesses related to the skills and experience required for the job. Focus on building on your strengths and addressing your weaknesses through training or seeking guidance from others.

2.Personal Development:

If you're looking to develop a new skill or hobby, identify your strengths and weaknesses in that area. Focus on building on your strengths and addressing your weaknesses through practice and seeking feedback from others who are more skilled in that area.

3.Relationship Building:

If you're looking to build stronger relationships with others, identify your strengths and weaknesses in communication and interpersonal skills. Focus on building on your strengths, such as active listening or empathy, and addressing your weaknesses, such as conflict resolution or assertiveness.

4.Health and Fitness:

If you're looking to improve your health and fitness, identify your strengths and weaknesses in areas such as nutrition, exercise, and mental health. Focus on building on your strengths, such as consistency in exercise or healthy meal planning, and addressing your weaknesses, such as stress management or sleep habits.

5.Entrepreneurship:

If you're looking to start your own business, identify your strengths and weaknesses in areas such as creativity, leadership, and financial management. Focus on building on your strengths and seeking support or education to address your weaknesses, such as taking a course on accounting or seeking guidance from a mentor.

Conclusion

Identifying your strengths and weaknesses is a crucial step in living up to your full potential. By understanding your unique talents and areas for improvement, you can focus your efforts on areas where you excel and take steps to address your weaknesses. This can help you achieve your goals, whether they are related to personal growth, career advancement, or health and wellness.

Remember that identifying your weaknesses can be difficult, but it's important to be honest with yourself and seek feedback from others. Don't be afraid to seek support or guidance from a mentor or coach as you work to develop your skills and reach your full potential. With dedication and a growth mindset, you can achieve great things and live up to your fullest potential.

A very old and wise individual who is still very successful but chooses to be nameless once told me "that the key to succession when considering your strengths and weaknesses is to surround yourself with the very people that carry the strengths to your weakness', they can make your life a lot easier, but if you can carry the strengths to their weaknesses, the cost of learning from each other is priceless for the both of you which is a great investment of time spent. Never let your ego get in the way of your humility, you will see that stronger relations can be forged."

This chapter might have been a little repetitive but there is a means to that madness. There is a great strength in repetition, it's the gift of memory retention, a very powerful skill to possess in this world. You may experience more of this in the upcoming chapters.

I want you to thrive, I want you to win, the greatest joy I have in this world is helping people become their greatest versions. This is a part of me living to my full potential, it's my purpose. This is where my strengths reside. This is where my heart feels full.

FS

Chapter 3
Setting Realistic
Goals

In order to live up to your full potential, it's important to set goals that are challenging yet achievable. Setting realistic goals can help you stay focused, motivated, and track your progress. In this chapter, we will explore why setting realistic goals is important, how to set effective goals, and how to stay motivated throughout the process.

SMART goals were developed by George Doran, Arthur Miller and James Cunningham in their 1981 article "There's a S.M.A.R.T. way to write management goals and objectives" . Since then an extra E and an R were added that prove to stand the test of time.

Specific, Measurable, Attainable, Realistic and Timely , Evaluate, Readjust (SMARTER)

Why Set Realistic Goals?

How To Utilize Your Full Potential

Setting realistic goals is important for several reasons:

1.Motivation: Setting realistic goals can help you stay motivated and focused on achieving what you want. When goals are too easy, you may not feel motivated to push yourself, and when they're too difficult, you may feel discouraged or overwhelmed.

2.Accountability: Setting realistic goals can help you hold yourself accountable for your progress. When you set achievable goals, you can track your progress and adjust your approach if needed.

3.Time Management:
Setting realistic goals can also help you manage your time more effectively. By breaking down large goals into smaller, more achievable steps, you can make progress towards your goals without feeling overwhelmed or stressed.

How to Set Effective Goals
When setting goals, it's important to follow these key steps:

1.Identify Your Objective:
The first step in setting goals is to identify what you want to achieve. This may be related to your personal life, career, health, or any other area of your life.

2.Make it SPECIFIC:
Once you have identified your objective, make your goal specific. This means defining what you want to achieve in clear and concise terms.What are you trying to do? Who is going to be part of the team? Why are you trying to do this? Where is what you are trying to do taking place? When will you do what you need to do? Be specific, provide a clear picture and hold people accountable.

3.Make it MEASURABLE:

Your goal should be measurable, which means defining specific metrics or milestones that will help you track your progress. How will you measure what you are doing? Is it by the number of people attending an event, the number of people navigating your webpage? How will you assess your achievement?

4.Make it ATTAINABLE:

Your goal should be challenging yet attainable. This means considering your current skill set, resources, and any other factors that may impact your ability to achieve your goal. With the tools that you have can you reach your goal? If not, what do you need? If you are trying to fundraise to buy winter coats for two-hundred children, can you obtain the amount of money needed to purchase the coats, can you find donors or establish a partnership with a local store?

5.Make it RELEVANT:

Your goal should be relevant to your overall objectives and values. This means considering why this goal is important to you and how it aligns with your long-term aspirations. Can you actually meet the goals you are setting forth? Using the same example: if you only have three people in your organization, how much time and effort can the three of you give in order to fundraise for two hundred coats? If the objective is not realistic, what do you need to do to make it so or do you need to change the objective?

6.Make it TIMELY:

Your goal should be time-bound, which means setting specific progress checkpoints to complete or setting a deadline for achieving it. What is the timeline to meet your goals? Work backwards. Start with your final objective and backwards plan to create an outline. Backwards planning gives the big picture and helps identify all that needs to get done. Logistics can be tricky: transportation, room reservations, requisitions, purchases, advertising all require work in advance.

Goal setting can be daunting but can be key when executing a project. Once accomplished, goal setting provides a place for reflection and to identify areas for future growth or change.

7.Make an EVALUATION:

Continuously evaluate your goals all the way along the process. This can differ by person. Some people may want to evaluate the progress of their goal daily, some weekly and some bi-monthly. Whatever you prefer, make sure you are continuously evaluating your goals to help make sure you achieve them. This goal links very well with timely, in that you have a timeline-based approach to goal setting.It also means evaluating your performance at the end of the process so that you can learn from your mistakes and optimize your next goal setting.

8.READJUST:

 Ever been faced with a continuous problem in the workplace, are you hitting the wall? Well this letter is here to help you. If you are facing a continuous problem with your goals, it's time to take a step back and re-adjust. Re-adjusting doesn't mean throwing away the goals and getting new ones, it's a means to an end, a way of getting around your problems.

How To Utilize Your Full Potential

Why Set Goals?

Goal setting can:
• Add value to the work that you are doing
• Help disseminate the workload more evenly
• Allow you to assess your progress along the way
• Help you figure out how to move forward if you encounter drawbacks
• Manage your time more effectively which can diminish burn out or needless work for you or your group
• Establish what you are trying to accomplish
• Clarify the definition of success
• Develop clear purpose which can help with recruitment of volunteers or community partners
• Inform budget development and, identification of resources
• Demonstrate that your organization is going to provide manageable tasks
• Help you work smarter not harder

Staying Motivated to Achieve Your Goals

(I repeat) Setting realistic goals is only the first step towards achieving what you want. Staying motivated and committed to your goals is essential.

Here are some tips to help you stay motivated:

1.Break it Down:
Break your larger goal into smaller, more manageable steps. This can help you make progress without feeling overwhelmed.

How To Utilize Your Full Potential

2.Celebrate Progress: Celebrate your progress along the way, no matter how small. This can help you stay motivated and focused on the bigger picture.

3.Stay Accountable:

Find someone who can hold you accountable for your progress, whether it's a friend, family member, or coach.

4.Visualize Success:

Visualize yourself achieving your goal and how it will feel when you reach it. This can help you stay motivated and focused on your end goal.

5.Adjust as Needed:

Don't be afraid to adjust your approach if needed. Sometimes, our goals may need to be adjusted based on new information or unforeseen challenges.

Examples of Realistic Goal Setting

Here are some examples of setting realistic goals in different areas of life:

1.Career:

A realistic goal for career advancement might be to obtain a new certification or degree within a specific timeframe.

2.Health:

A realistic goal for improving your health might be to lose a certain amount of weight within a reasonable timeframe or to exercise for a specific amount of time each week.

3.Personal Growth:

A realistic goal for personal growth might be to read a certain number of books on a particular topic within a specific timeframe.

4.Relationship Building:

A realistic goal for relationship building might be to schedule regular quality time with a loved one, such as a weekly dinner or a monthly outing.

5.Financial:

A realistic goal for financial stability might be to save a certain amount of money each month or to pay off a specific debt within a specific timeframe.

6.When setting goals, it's important to consider your current resources, skills, and priorities. Don't set yourself up for failure by setting unrealistic or unattainable goals. Be honest with yourself about what you can realistically achieve, and don't be afraid to adjust your goals as needed.

7.Another important aspect of setting goals is to make sure they are aligned with your values and aspirations. If you're setting goals that don't truly resonate with you or align with your long-term goals, it can be difficult to stay motivated and committed to achieving them.

8.It's also important to remember that setbacks and obstacles are a natural part of the goal-setting process. Don't let them discourage you or make you feel like you've failed. Use them as opportunities to learn and adjust your approach.

In summary, setting realistic goals is crucial for living up to your full potential. It can help you stay motivated, hold yourself accountable, and manage your time more effectively. Follow the SMARTER key steps of goal setting, stay motivated, and adjust as needed. By setting achievable goals that align with your values and aspirations, you can take concrete steps towards living the life you want.

To get realistic with you it took me many years to master this and even now I still tend to forget to evaluate and readjust or get things done in a timely manner because things happen, life happens.

I get to a point where I want something so badly that I'll stop at nothing to achieve it and it turns me into this trudging horse with blinders on and not caring for the things that do not go completely right, I've gotten stuck in hoping they'll just sort themselves out!

After all, I'm only human. I make errors, I still have compassion for myself, my stubbornness and commitment are like an ebb and flow of desired goals and the intense passion to achieve them. Once everything that should be going right keeps going wrong, I question my sanity and reasoning of why I'm allowing it to unfold that way and then decide to go for a walk because I've said my last "F-this!" and now crave balance and some inspiration with fresh air to reach this thick skull. I go into a meditative state clearing myself of all of the transgressions, do some 4-fold breathing, I'll add it in here, you can walk and meditate too you know, focusing on what one great achievement would look like in the mind's eye like me getting this book done for example.

Wait till you see the rabbit hole I take you down in book 2, it's going to change your whole perspective on life and succeeding!

So let's keep going. We're not even half way after all.

Don't forget the acronym SMARTER and its attributes its the elephant in the room when considering this chapter and that's the whole goal of this book, it's to make you a smarter, more calculated, confidant and a more empowered individual who can pick up all the years of useful wisdom faster than it took me through my experiences, living towards your FULL POTENTIAL!!!

FS

Chapter 4
Overcoming Fear
And
Limiting Beliefs

Fear is a natural human emotion that can hold us back from living our full potential. It can prevent us from taking risks, pursuing our passions, and reaching our goals. However, overcoming fear is essential for personal growth and development.

The first step in overcoming fear is to acknowledge and understand it. Identify the source of your fear and examine how it affects your thoughts and behaviors. Recognize that fear is often rooted in negative beliefs or past experiences, and challenge those beliefs with positive affirmations and self-talk.

Next, take small steps towards facing your fears. Break down your goals into manageable tasks and take action towards them. This will help build confidence and momentum.

Another helpful strategy is to seek support from others. Talk to trusted friends, family members, or a therapist about your fears and goals. They can provide encouragement, guidance, and accountability.

In summary, overcoming fear requires acknowledging it with perseverance and dedication. You can break free from the limitations of fear and live your full potential.

Limiting beliefs are the thoughts and attitudes that hold us back from achieving our full potential. These beliefs can be conscious or unconscious, and they often stem from past experiences or conditioning. In this chapter, we will explore how to identify and overcome limiting beliefs so that we can reach our full potential.

Identifying Limiting Beliefs

The first step in overcoming limiting beliefs is to identify them.

Limiting beliefs can manifest in many ways, such as:

• Negative self-talk:
Thoughts like "I'm not good enough," "I can't do this," or "Success is too far and takes too long to reach," are examples of negative self-talk that can hold us back.

• Fear of failure:
A fear of failure can prevent us from taking risks or pursuing our goals.

• Fear of success:
A fear of success can also hold us back, as we may be afraid of the responsibilities or changes that come with success.

• Comparison to others:
Comparing ourselves to others and feeling like we don't measure up can be a form of limiting belief.

How To Utilize Your Full Potential

• Beliefs about money:

Beliefs about money, such as "money is the root of all evil" or "rich people are greedy," can prevent us from achieving financial success.

Once you identify your limiting beliefs, it's important to understand where they come from. Did they stem from past experiences, family upbringing, societal conditioning, or something else?

Understanding the root of your limiting beliefs can help you overcome them.

Challenging Limiting Beliefs

The next step in overcoming limiting beliefs is to challenge them. This means questioning the validity of these beliefs and looking for evidence to support or disprove them.

Here are some strategies to help you challenge your limiting beliefs:

1. Write it down:

Write down your limiting belief and the evidence that supports or disproves it. For example, if your limiting belief is "I'm not good enough," write down times when you succeeded in something, no matter how small.

2. Ask yourself questions:

Ask yourself questions like "Is this belief true?" or "What evidence do I have to support this belief?" This can help you see your limiting beliefs from a more objective perspective.

3.Reframe your thoughts:

Instead of focusing on the negative aspects of a situation, reframe your thoughts in a positive way. For example, instead of thinking "I can't do this," reframe it as "I haven't done this yet, but I'm willing to try."

4.Practice self-compassion:

Be kind to yourself and recognize that it's okay to make mistakes or experience setbacks. Practice self-compassion by treating yourself with the same kindness and understanding you would give to a loved family member or a good friend.

5.Seek support:

Talk to a trusted friend, family member, or professional about your limiting beliefs. They can offer a different perspective and help you see things in a more positive light.

Overcoming Limiting Beliefs

Overcoming limiting beliefs is not a one-time event, but rather a continuous process.

Here are some additional strategies to help you overcome limiting beliefs and reach your full potential:

1.Visualize Success: Visualize yourself succeeding and achieving your goals. This can help you overcome limiting beliefs and stay motivated towards achieving what you want.

2.Practice Positive Self-Talk:

Practice positive self-talk by reminding yourself of your strengths, skills, and accomplishments.

3.Take Action:

Take action towards your goals, even if it's just a small step. This can help build momentum and confidence.

4.Surround Yourself with Positivity:

Surround yourself with positive people and environments that support your growth and development.

5.Embrace Failure:

Embrace failure as a natural part of the learning process. Use it as an opportunity to learn, grow, and improve.

In summary

Overcoming limiting beliefs is a critical step in reaching your full potential. These beliefs can hold you back from pursuing your passions, taking risks, and achieving your goals. By challenging these beliefs and taking action towards your goals, you can overcome them and unlock your full potential.

It's important to remember that overcoming limiting beliefs is not always easy. It can be a difficult and an uncomfortable process, as you may need to confront and challenge deeply ingrained beliefs about yourself and the world around you. However, by staying committed and taking small steps towards your goals, you can gradually overcome these limiting beliefs and achieve your full potential.

One useful tool for overcoming limiting beliefs is to create a growth mindset. A growth mindset is the belief that your abilities and intelligence can be developed through hard work, practice, and dedication. This mindset can help you approach challenges with a positive attitude and view failure as an opportunity to learn and grow.

Another important aspect of overcoming limiting beliefs is to develop a sense of self-awareness. By understanding your thoughts, emotions, and behaviors, you can identify patterns of negative self-talk or self-sabotage that may be holding you back. This awareness can help you challenge these beliefs and make changes that support your growth and development.

Finally, it's important to celebrate your successes along the way. Recognize and acknowledge your progress, no matter how small, and use it as motivation to keep pushing forward. Overcoming limiting beliefs is a journey, and celebrating your successes can help you stay motivated and focused on your goals.

In conclusion, identifying and overcoming fear and limiting beliefs is an essential step in pursuing your full potential. By challenging these beliefs, developing a growth mindset, and staying committed to your goals, you can unlock your full potential and achieve success in all areas of your life. Remember to be patient, kind to yourself, and celebrate your successes along the way.

Chapter 5
Cultivating A Positive Mindset

One of the most important factors in achieving your full potential is your mindset. A positive mindset can help you approach challenges with confidence and resilience, while a negative mindset can hold you back and lead to self-doubt and limiting beliefs. In this chapter, we will explore the importance of cultivating a positive mindset and provide practical tips for doing so.

The Difference between a fixed and growth mindsets

Fixed and growth mindsets are two different ways of thinking about one's abilities and potential.

A fixed mindset is the belief that intelligence, talent, and ability are innate and cannot be changed. Individuals with a fixed mindset believe that their qualities are fixed and cannot be developed through effort or learning. They may avoid challenges, give up easily, or feel threatened by the success of others.

In contrast, a growth mindset is the belief that intelligence, talent, and ability can be developed through hard work, dedication, and learning. Individuals with a growth mindset embrace challenges, persist in the face of obstacles, and are inspired by the success of others.

The difference between fixed and growth mindsets has important implications for personal and professional development. Individuals with a fixed mindset may limit their potential by avoiding challenges, giving up easily, or not seeking opportunities for growth. In contrast, individuals with a growth mindset are more likely to embrace challenges, take risks, and seek out opportunities for growth and development.

It is important to note that fixed and growth mindsets are not absolute, and individuals may exhibit elements of both mindsets in different contexts. However, cultivating a growth mindset can lead to greater personal and professional success, as it promotes resilience, persistence, and a willingness to learn and grow.

The first step in cultivating a positive mindset is to practice gratitude.

Gratitude is the practice of recognizing and appreciating the good things in your life, no matter how small. By focusing on the positive aspects of your life, you can shift your mindset from one of negativity and self-doubt to one of positivity and abundance.

To practice gratitude, try starting a daily gratitude journal. Each day, write down three things you are grateful for, no matter how small or seemingly insignificant. By doing this, you will train your mind to focus on the positive aspects of your life and develop a more positive outlook overall.

Another important aspect of cultivating a positive mindset is to practice self-compassion. Self-compassion involves treating yourself with kindness and understanding, particularly in moments of struggle or difficulty. By practicing self-compassion, you can develop a more positive relationship with yourself and cultivate a sense of inner peace and self-acceptance.

To practice self-compassion, try speaking to yourself in the same way you would speak to a loved family member or a close friend who is going through a difficult time. Offer words of encouragement and support, rather than criticism or self-blame. By doing this, you can develop a more positive and nurturing relationship with yourself.

Finally, (I repeat yet again) it's important to cultivate a growth mindset. A growth mindset is the belief that your abilities and intelligence can be developed through hard work, practice, and dedication. By developing a growth mindset, you can approach challenges with a sense of curiosity and a willingness to learn, rather than a sense of defeat or inadequacy.

To cultivate a growth mindset, try reframing your thoughts about challenges and setbacks. Instead of viewing them as failures or signs of inadequacy, view them as opportunities to learn and grow. Ask yourself what you can learn from the experience and how you can use that knowledge to improve in the future.

In conclusion, cultivating a positive mindset is essential for achieving your full potential. By practicing gratitude, self-compassion, and a growth mindset, you can develop a more positive outlook and approach challenges with confidence and resilience.

Remember to be patient and kind to yourself, and celebrate your successes along the way. With a positive mindset, you can achieve anything you set your mind to.

Chapter 6

Finding Your

Purpose

To live a fulfilling and satisfying life, it's important to find your purpose. Your purpose is your reason for being, the thing that gives your life meaning and direction. It's what makes you feel alive, passionate, and fulfilled. In this chapter, we will explore the importance of finding your purpose and provide practical tips for doing so.

The first step in finding your purpose is to identify your passions and interests.

Think about the things that excite and inspire you, and the activities that you enjoy most. This could be anything from painting or writing to working with animals, building things or helping other people, the possibilities are endless . Once you have identified your passions, you can start to explore how you can incorporate them into your life and work.

Finding a profession is really easy in this day and age of the information era with so much information online at your fingertips. Whatever it may be you will find someone online who is great at their profession showcasing their skill and it's all there for you to learn from.

How To Utilize Your Full Potential

Another important aspect of finding your purpose is to identify your values and beliefs.

What is important to you?
What do you stand for?
What do you believe in?

Your values and beliefs will guide you in making important decisions and help you stay true to yourself and your purpose.

It can also be helpful to reflect on your past experiences and achievements.

What have been some of the most fulfilling and satisfying moments in your life?

What were you doing, and how did it make you feel?

By identifying the experiences and achievements that have brought you the most joy and satisfaction, you can start to see patterns and themes that can help guide you towards your purpose.

Once you have a clear idea of your passions, values, and past experiences, you can start to create a purpose statement. This is a statement that defines your purpose in life, and should be clear, concise, and inspiring. It should reflect your passions, values, and beliefs, and provide a sense of direction and meaning for your life.

For example :
My purpose is to help people in becoming independently successful. At the beginning I will challenge their thinking by exposing their negative points to help them become more self-aware, guide them to conquer their negative obstacles and clear any blockages

they may have. I help them create an action plan and hold them accountable to meet their chosen goals and navigate through their obstacles in whatever they wish to become. I find value in people even when they can't see it. I have battled self-worth issues for years and have found the power to overcome them and now know that anyone can overcome them with the right mindset. I am passionate about sharing insight and wisdom I've attained with my positive and negative experiences in life that could potentially motivate and inspire someone to succeed.

To live your purpose, it's important to take action. This means setting goals and taking steps towards achieving them. It can also mean finding ways to incorporate your purpose into your work, hobbies, and daily life. By taking action and living your purpose, you will feel more fulfilled, satisfied, and energized.

Finally, it's important to stay open to new experiences and opportunities. Your purpose may evolve and change over time, and it's important to be versatile, flexible and adaptable. By staying open to new ideas and experiences, you can continue to grow and evolve, and live a life that is true to your purpose.

In conclusion, finding your purpose is an important step in living a fulfilling and satisfying life. By identifying your passions, values, and past experiences, creating a purpose statement, taking action, and staying open to new experiences, you can discover your purpose and live a life that is true to your values and passions.

Remember, your purpose may evolve and change over time, and it's important to stay versatile, flexible and adaptable. With patience, persistence, and an open mind, you can find your purpose and live a life that is truly meaningful and fulfilling.

Chapter 7
Taking Action

In Chapter 6, we discussed the importance of finding your purpose and how it can guide you towards living up to your full potential. But finding your purpose alone is not enough; you also need to take action towards achieving your goals and realizing your potential. In this chapter, we will explore the importance of taking action and provide practical tips for making progress towards your goals.

Taking action is the key to making progress towards your goals and achieving success. It means turning your ideas and dreams into tangible actions and results. But taking action can be challenging, especially when faced with obstacles or uncertainty. That's why it's important to develop a mindset of action, which means being proactive, persistent, and adaptable.

Firstly we will discuss procrastination. It has become worse than a pandemic in this day and age.

Strategies for Procrastination.

Procrastination is a common problem that many people face, and it can have negative effects on productivity and well-being.

How To Utilize Your Full Potential

Here are some strategies for overcoming procrastination:

1.Break tasks into smaller pieces:
Often, the thought of completing a large task can be overwhelming and lead to procrastination. Breaking the task into smaller, more manageable pieces can make it easier to get started.

2.Set specific goals and deadlines:
 Setting clear goals and deadlines can help provide motivation and a sense of direction. Make sure your goals are realistic and achievable, and create a timeline for completing them.

3.Eliminate distractions:
Distractions such as social media or television can interfere with productivity and make it easier to procrastinate. Identify potential distractions and create a workspace that minimizes them.

4.Use positive self-talk:
Negative self-talk can be a barrier to getting things done. Use positive self-talk to build confidence and motivate yourself to take action.

5.Prioritize tasks:
Prioritizing tasks can help you focus on the most important tasks and avoid procrastinating on less important ones.

6.Take breaks:
 It's important to take breaks throughout the day to recharge and avoid burnout. However, make sure your breaks are planned and don't turn into prolonged distractions.

7.Use the "two-minute rule":

If a task takes less than two minutes to complete, do it immediately. This can help build momentum and make it easier to tackle more challenging tasks.

Remember that overcoming procrastination takes practice and persistence. By implementing these strategies, you can start to break the cycle of procrastination and increase your action that leads to productivity and proactiveness.

Taking imperfect Action

Taking imperfect action means taking action even if the plan is not perfect or the outcome is uncertain. It is a mindset that focuses on progress rather than perfection. Here are some benefits of taking imperfect action:

1.Overcome fear and build confidence:

Fear of failure or uncertainty can hold us back from taking action. By taking imperfect action, we can confront and overcome our fears, building confidence in our abilities and decision-making.

2.Learn from mistakes:

Imperfect action allows us to make mistakes, and mistakes are an opportunity to learn and grow. By taking action, we gain valuable feedback on what works and what doesn't, which can help us improve and refine our approach.

3.Increase productivity:

Waiting for the perfect plan or outcome can lead to analysis paralysis, which can prevent progress. By taking imperfect action, we can break out of this cycle and start making progress towards our goals.

4.Adapt to change:

In today's rapidly changing world, plans and strategies can quickly become outdated. Taking imperfect action can help us stay agile and adapt to changing circumstances, allowing us to pivot and adjust our approach as needed.

5.Create momentum:

Taking action, even imperfect action, can create momentum and a sense of progress. This can help us stay motivated and focused on our goals, leading to further progress and success.

6.Gain clarity:

Often, we don't know what we don't know until we start taking action. Imperfect action can help us gain clarity on our goals, priorities, and what is working or not working.

7.Avoid missed opportunities:

Waiting for the perfect plan or outcome can cause us to miss opportunities that are time-sensitive or require quick action. Imperfect action can help us seize opportunities and capitalize on them.

In conclusion, taking imperfect action can have many benefits, including overcoming fear, learning from mistakes, increasing productivity, adapting to change, creating momentum, gaining clarity, and avoiding missed opportunities. By embracing imperfect action, we can move closer to our goals and achieve greater success.

Being proactive means taking the initiative to create opportunities and take action towards your goals. It means not waiting for opportunities to come to you, but actively seeking them out and creating your own. This can be as simple as reaching out to someone for advice or networking, or as ambitious as launching a new business or pursuing a new career.

How To Utilize Your Full Potential

Being persistent means staying committed to your goals, even in the face of challenges and setbacks. It means not giving up when things get tough, but instead, finding ways to overcome obstacles and keep moving forward. This can be achieved by breaking down your goals into smaller, achievable steps, and taking consistent action towards each step.

Being adaptable means being flexible and open to change. It means being willing to adjust your approach if necessary, and to learn from your mistakes and failures. This can be achieved by being open to feedback and constructive criticism, and by being willing to try new approaches and experiment with different strategies.

One effective way to take action towards your goals is to create a plan.

This can be a detailed action plan or a simple to-do list, but it should outline the specific steps you need to take to reach your goals. By breaking down your goals into smaller steps, you can make them more manageable and less overwhelming, and increase your chances of success.

Another important aspect of taking action towards your goals is to stay focused and motivated. This means staying committed to your goals, even when faced with challenges or setbacks. It can also mean finding ways to stay motivated and inspired, such as surrounding yourself with supportive people, visualizing your success, or rewarding yourself for achieving milestones.

It's also important to stay accountable to yourself and others. This means tracking your progress towards your goals, celebrating your achievements, and being honest with yourself about any setbacks or challenges you may face. It can also mean finding an accountability partner or support group, who can provide motivation and encouragement along the way.

In conclusion, taking action towards your goals is essential for living up to your full potential. By developing a mindset of action, creating a plan, staying focused and motivated, and staying accountable to yourself and others, you can make progress towards your goals and achieve success.

Remember, taking action requires effort, persistence, and a willingness to adapt, but with patience and dedication, you can achieve anything you set your mind to.

Chapter 8
Embracing Failure
And
Learning From Mistakes

Many of us fear failure and avoid taking risks because we don't want to experience the pain of falling short of our goals. However, the truth is that failure is an inevitable part of any journey towards success and living up to our full potential.

In fact, embracing failure and learning from our mistakes is a key component of growth and development. In this chapter, we will explore the importance of embracing failure and learning from mistakes, and provide tips for how to do so effectively.

One of the main reasons why failure is so important for growth is that it provides valuable feedback and learning opportunities. When we fail, we have the chance to reflect on what went wrong, identify areas for improvement, and adjust our approach for future attempts. This process of reflection and adjustment is essential for developing new skills, refining our strategies, and ultimately achieving success.

Moreover, failure can also help us build resilience and develop a growth mindset. When we experience setbacks or failures, it's easy to feel discouraged and give up on our goals.

However, by embracing failure as a natural part of the learning process, we can develop a more positive outlook and a greater sense of resilience. This means being able to bounce back from setbacks, stay motivated, and keep pushing towards our goals.

So how can we embrace failure and learn from our mistakes effectively? Here are a few tips:

1.Shift your mindset:
Instead of seeing failure as a negative outcome, reframe it as an opportunity for growth and learning. Recognize that failure is a natural part of the process and that it provides valuable feedback for future attempts.

2.Reflect on your mistakes:
When you experience failure, take some time to reflect on what went wrong and why. Consider what factors may have contributed to the failure and identify areas for improvement.

3.Adjust your approach:
Once you've identified areas for improvement, adjust your approach accordingly. This may mean trying a new strategy, seeking additional support, or simply making small tweaks to your existing plan.

4.Stay motivated:
Remember that setbacks and failures are a normal part of the journey towards success. Stay motivated by focusing on your long-term goals, surrounding yourself with

supportive people, and celebrating small victories along the way.

5.Practice self-compassion:
It's important to be kind and compassionate towards yourself, especially when experiencing setbacks or failures. Recognize that failure does not define your worth or abilities, and be gentle with yourself as you work towards your goals.

It's also important to recognize that failure is not always the result of our own shortcomings. External factors, such as unexpected challenges or changes in circumstances, can also contribute to failure. In these cases, it's important to acknowledge that failure is not always within our control and to focus on what we can do to move forward.

In conclusion, embracing failure and learning from mistakes is a critical component of growth and development.

By shifting our mindset, reflecting on our mistakes, adjusting our approach, staying motivated, and practicing self-compassion, we can effectively embrace failure and use it as a springboard for success.

Remember, failure is not the end of the road, but rather a necessary step on the journey towards realizing our full potential.

Chapter 9

Building A

Support System

Living up to our full potential is not always an easy journey, and it's important to have a strong support system in place to help us navigate the ups and downs along the way. A support system can provide encouragement, guidance, and accountability, as well as a sense of belonging and connection. In this chapter, we will explore the importance of building a support system and provide tips for how to do so effectively.

First and foremost, it's important to recognize that building a support system is not a one-size-fits-all approach. The type of support system that works best for you will depend on your personality, goals, and preferences. Some people may prefer a large network of friends and family members, while others may prefer a smaller group of close confidants.

Regardless of the specifics, there are a few key components that should be included in any effective support system:

How To Utilize Your Full Potential

1.Positive and supportive people:

The people in your support system should be positive and supportive, providing encouragement and motivation when you need it most.

2.Accountability partners:

Accountability partners can help keep you on track towards your goals by holding you accountable and providing feedback when necessary.

3.Mentors or advisors:

Mentors or advisors can provide guidance and expertise in areas where you may need support or direction.

4.Professional support:

Professional support, such as therapy or coaching, can also be an important part of your support system, providing additional resources and expertise.

Once you have an idea of the types of people you want in your support system, the next step is to start building those relationships.

Here are a few tips for building a strong support system:

1.Be intentional:

Building a support system takes time and effort, so it's important to be intentional about who you want in your network and how you want to develop those relationships.

2.Seek out like-minded individuals:

Look for people who share similar interests, goals, or values. These individuals are more likely to understand your journey and provide the support you need.

3.Be vulnerable:
Building strong relationships requires vulnerability and openness. Be willing to share your struggles and challenges with those in your support system, and be receptive to feedback and advice.

4.Offer support in return:
Building a support system is a two-way street. Be willing to provide support and encouragement to others in your network, as well as seek it out for yourself.

5.Maintain communication:
Consistent communication is key to building and maintaining strong relationships. Make time to check in with those in your support system regularly, whether through phone calls, text messages, or in-person meetings.

It's also important to remember that building a support system is not a one-time event, but rather an ongoing process.

As your goals and needs change over time, your support system may need to evolve as well. It's important to stay open to new relationships and opportunities for support as they arise.

In addition to building a support system, it's also important to cultivate a sense of community and connection more broadly. This can involve participating in group activities or organizations that align with your interests or goals, or simply finding ways to connect with others in your community.

Having a strong support system and sense of community can be incredibly beneficial for living up to your full potential. Not only can it provide encouragement and motivation, but it can also help you stay accountable, gain new perspectives, and build resilience in the face of challenges.

So, take the time to invest in your relationships and build a support system that will help you thrive. In fact, finding a way to cultivate each other to thrive will fortify these relationships for many years ahead.

The benefits of having a mentor or a coach

Having a mentor or coach is essential in helping individuals live up to their full potential.

A mentor is someone who has more experience, knowledge, and expertise in a particular field than the person they are mentoring.

A coach, on the other hand, is someone who helps individuals set goals, develop skills, and overcome obstacles to achieve success in their personal or professional lives.There are several reasons why having a mentor or coach is crucial in living up to your full potential.

Firstly, they can provide guidance and advice on how to navigate challenging situations. Whether it is a difficult project at work or a personal struggle, a mentor or coach can offer insights based on their own experiences and help individuals develop effective solutions.

Secondly, a mentor or coach can help individuals identify their strengths and weaknesses. By understanding their strengths, individuals can leverage them to achieve greater success, while understanding their weaknesses can help them develop strategies to overcome them.

Thirdly, a mentor or coach can provide accountability and motivation. They can help individuals set achievable goals and provide support and encouragement to help them stay on track. This accountability and motivation can be especially helpful during times of uncertainty or doubt.

Finally, a mentor or coach can provide opportunities for growth and development. By introducing individuals to new ideas, perspectives, and experiences, mentors and coaches can help them expand their knowledge and skills, and develop new abilities that will help them reach their full potential.

In conclusion, having a mentor or coach is essential in helping individuals live up to their full potential. They provide guidance, support, and motivation, and help individuals develop the skills and abilities they need to succeed in their personal and professional lives.

Chapter 10
Self-Care, Self-Love
Loving Others And Balance

Living up to your full potential requires not only hard work and dedication but also taking care of yourself. Self-care is an essential component of achieving your goals and living a fulfilling life.

In this chapter, we will explore the importance of self-care and provide tips for how to incorporate it into your daily routine.

Self-care involves taking deliberate actions to care for your physical, emotional, and mental health. It's about prioritizing your well-being and making choices that support your overall health and happiness. Self-care looks different for everyone, and it's important to find what works best for you.
Here are some common strategies for self-care:

1. Prioritizing sleep:
Getting enough sleep is crucial for your physical and mental health. Aim for at least 7-8 hours of sleep per night, and create a relaxing bedtime routine to help you unwind and prepare for rest.

2. Eating a healthy diet:

Eating a balanced diet that includes plenty of fruits, vegetables, and lean protein can provide you with the energy and nutrients you need to perform at your best.

3. Regular exercise:

Physical activity not only helps to keep you physically healthy but also provides numerous mental health benefits. Find an activity that you enjoy, whether it's running, yoga, or hiking, and aim for at least 30 minutes of exercise per day.

4. Mindfulness practices:

Mindfulness practices such as meditation, yoga, or deep breathing exercises can help reduce stress and anxiety, improve focus and concentration, and promote overall well-being.

5. Social connection:

Building and maintaining relationships with others can provide a sense of community and belonging, which is important for overall well-being. Make time for social activities and prioritize spending time with loved ones.

6. Positive spiritual practices:

Created of your own choosing be it of an ancestral nature or a religious nature that you can completely convince yourself that you are working in an alignment with a higher power or energy in achieving your better purpose. The energy that you are is your soul that animates the body you are in that comes with an ego that you identify as. Your soul comes from an all-encompassing and infinite source with unlimited energy, the ego is only a part of the body connected to the psyche.

How To Utilize Your Full Potential

The Ego and how to control it

The ego, in psychology, refers to the part of the human psyche that is responsible for self-awareness, identity, and personal agency. It is the mediator between the inner self and the external world. It is responsible for our sense of self-esteem, self-worth, and self-confidence. The ego can be both helpful and harmful, depending on how it is controlled and managed. Here are some ways to control the ego:

1.Understand the nature of the ego:
The ego is not inherently good or bad; it is simply a part of the human psyche. Understanding the nature of the ego and its role in our lives is the first step in controlling it.

2.Observe your thoughts:
The ego often manifests itself in our thoughts. By observing our thoughts and recognizing when they are ego-driven, we can take steps to control them.

3. Practice mindfulness:
Mindfulness is the practice of being fully present and aware of your thoughts and surroundings. By practicing mindfulness, we can become more aware of our ego and learn to control it.

4.Cultivate humility:
Humility is the opposite of ego. By cultivating humility, we can learn to put the needs of others before our own and recognize that we are not the center of the universe.

5.Practice self-awareness:
Self-awareness is the ability to recognize and understand your emotions, thoughts, and

behaviors. By practicing self-awareness, we can become more in tune with our ego and learn to control it.

6.Focus on your values:

Focusing on your values can help you keep your ego in check. When we focus on our values, we are less likely to be driven by our ego and more likely to act in accordance with our true selves.

7.Seek feedback:

Feedback from others can be a valuable tool in controlling the ego. By seeking feedback, we can gain a better understanding of how our ego is impacting our relationships and behavior.

In conclusion, the ego is an integral part of the human psyche. By understanding its nature and practicing self-awareness, mindfulness, humility, and focusing on our values, we can learn to control it and use it in a positive way.

Incorporating self-care into your daily routine can be challenging, especially if you have a busy schedule or competing priorities.

Here are some tips for making self-care a regular part of your life:

1. Set boundaries:

It's important to set boundaries and prioritize your own needs. This may mean saying no to certain requests or commitments, or setting aside dedicated time for self-care activities .When we set boundaries, we show ourselves that we are in control of who or what energy's we allow to play a role in our daily lives to our self- development.

How To Utilize Your Full Potential

2. Schedule it in:
Treat self-care like any other important appointment by scheduling it into your calendar. This can help ensure that you prioritize self-care and make time for it regularly.

4. Make it enjoyable:
Self-care doesn't have to feel like a chore. Find activities that you enjoy and look forward to, whether it's taking a relaxing bath, a nice walk, hiking, a vacation, trying out a new exercise class or a workout at the gym.

5. Practice self-compassion:
It's easy to be hard on yourself when you feel like you're not doing enough, but it's important to practice self-compassion. Recognize that self-care is an ongoing process and be gentle with yourself as you work to incorporate it into your routine.

Taking care of yourself also means paying attention to your mental health. Mental health is an important component of overall well-being, and it's important to prioritize it just as you would your physical health.

Here are some strategies for promoting good mental health:

1. Seek help when needed:
If you're struggling with mental health issues such as anxiety or depression, it's important to seek help from a mental health professional. They can provide support and resources to help you manage your symptoms.

2. Practice stress management techniques:

Stress can have a negative impact on mental health. Practice stress management techniques such as meditation or deep breathing exercises to help reduce stress levels.

3. Build resilience:

Building resilience can help you better cope with challenges and setbacks. Focus on developing positive coping strategies such as problem-solving and positive self-talk.

4. Cultivate gratitude:

Cultivating gratitude can help you focus on the positive aspects of your life and promote overall well-being. Consider starting a gratitude journal or regularly practicing gratitude by reflecting on things you're thankful for.

5. Take breaks:

It's important to take breaks and give yourself time to rest and recharge. Whether it's taking a day off work or simply taking a few minutes to step away from a stressful situation, taking breaks can help prevent burnout and improve overall well-being.

Self love, love for others and self-balance

Self-love, love for others, and balance are interrelated concepts that are critical for personal growth and fulfillment. These three concepts are vital components of a healthy and balanced life. Self-love is the foundation upon which we build our self-esteem and self-confidence. It is the way we treat and value ourselves. Love for others is an extension of our self-love, as it allows us to give and receive love in a healthy and meaningful way. Finally, self-balance is the practice of finding equilibrium in all areas of our lives, including work, relationships, and personal growth. We will explore these concepts in-depth and provide practical tips for harnessing them in our daily lives.

Harnessing Self-Love:

Self-love is the practice of valuing and respecting yourself. It is the foundation for a healthy and fulfilling life. When we love ourselves, we are more confident, resilient, and empowered to pursue our goals and dreams. Here are some practical tips for harnessing self-love:

1.Practice Self-Care:
Self-care is the practice of taking care of our physical, emotional, and mental health. This includes getting enough sleep, exercising regularly, eating a healthy diet, and taking time to relax and unwind. When we take care of ourselves, we send a message to our subconscious that we are valuable and worthy of love.

2.Practice Positive Self-Talk:
Our internal dialogue can greatly influence how we feel about ourselves. When we engage in negative self-talk, we reinforce the idea that we are not good enough or worthy of love. On the other hand, positive self-talk can help us build self-esteem and confidence. Start by paying attention to your inner dialogue and challenging negative thoughts with positive affirmations

3.Embrace your uniqueness:
Each one of us is unique, with our strengths and weaknesses. We need to embrace our uniqueness and celebrate our individuality. Instead of comparing ourselves to others, we need to focus on our own journey and recognize our own accomplishments.

How To Utilize full Potential

Understanding Love for Others

Love for others is an essential component of a fulfilling life. It involves caring for and valuing the people in our lives, and cultivating meaningful and supportive relationships with them. Love for others can take many forms, including romantic love, familial love, friendship, and community.

Cultivating love for others requires empathy, compassion, and communication. Empathy involves understanding and sharing the feelings of others, and recognizing their unique perspectives and experiences. Compassion involves treating others with kindness, empathy, and understanding, especially in times of difficulty or challenge. Communication involves expressing our thoughts, feelings, and needs in a clear and respectful way, and listening to the thoughts, feelings, and needs of others.

Practicing love for others can enhance our mental, emotional, and physical health, and help us to create more meaningful and fulfilling relationships with others. It can improve our social support, reduce loneliness and isolation, and increase our sense of belonging and connection.

Understanding Balance

Balance is yet another key to a fulfilling life. It involves finding harmony and equilibrium between different aspects of our lives, including work, play, relationships, and self-care. Balance is not about achieving perfection or eliminating stress, but about managing our priorities and responsibilities in a way that honors our needs and values. Cultivating balance requires self-awareness, prioritization, and flexibility. Self-awareness involves understanding our needs, values, and goals, and recognizing the areas of our lives that may be out of balance. Prioritization involves identifying our top priorities and responsibilities, and allocating our time and energy accordingly. Flexibility involves adapting to unexpected changes or challenges, and making adjustments as needed to maintain balance. It can improve our productivity, creativity, and sense of fulfillment, and reduce stress, burnout, and overwhelm.

Emotional intelligence

Emotional intelligence (EI) is the ability to recognize, understand, and manage one's own emotions, as well as the emotions of others. It involves being able to identify and label different emotions, and to use this information to guide thinking and behavior. Emotional intelligence encompasses a range of skills, including self-awareness, self-regulation, motivation, empathy, and social skills.People with high emotional intelligence are able to recognize and regulate their own emotions, which helps them to cope with stress, make better decisions, and maintain positive relationships with others. They are also able to understand the emotions of others, which helps them to communicate effectively, resolve conflicts, and build strong relationships. Emotional intelligence is considered an important predictor of success in personal and professional life.

Here are some steps you can take to have and improve your emotional intelligence:

1. Recognize and label your emotions:
Start by becoming more aware of your emotions and giving them names. This helps you understand your emotional responses to situations and can help you manage them better.

2. Practice self-awareness:

Pay attention to your thoughts, feelings, and physical sensations in response to different situations. This helps you understand your emotional triggers and how to manage them.

3. Regulate your emotions:

Once you have identified your emotions, learn to regulate them effectively. This involves managing your emotions and responding appropriately to different situations.

4. Develop empathy:

Empathy is the ability to understand and share the feelings of others. Practice putting yourself in other people's shoes and try to see things from their perspective.

5. Practice active listening:

Pay attention to what others are saying, without interrupting or judging them. Try to understand their point of view and feelings.

6. Communicate effectively:

Improve your communication skills by expressing your own emotions clearly and effectively, and by using language that is respectful and empathetic.

7. Resolve conflicts constructively:

Learn to resolve conflicts in a calm and respectful way. Practice problem-solving skills and learn to negotiate in a way that meets everyone's needs.

8. Keep learning:
Continue learning about emotional intelligence, and practice what you learn in everyday life. Seek out resources, such as books, courses, and workshops, to help you improve your skills.

Remember that improving emotional intelligence is a continuous process. By practicing these steps, you can develop better self-awareness, regulate your emotions more effectively, and develop stronger relationships with others.

The benefits of mindfulness and meditation

Mindfulness and meditation are techniques that have been practiced for thousands of years and are known to provide a variety of benefits to one's physical, mental, and emotional well-being.

Mindfulness is the practice of being present and fully engaged in the moment, while meditation involves training the mind to focus and quieten itself.

One of the primary benefits of mindfulness and meditation is stress reduction. When practicing mindfulness or meditation, individuals learn to focus their attention on the present moment, which helps to reduce worry and anxiety about the past or future. This reduces the levels of the stress hormone cortisol, resulting in improved physical and emotional health.

Mindfulness and meditation can also improve focus and concentration. By training the mind to stay present, individuals can improve their ability to focus on the task at hand and be more productive in their daily lives.

How To Utilize Your Full Potential

Additionally, regular meditation practice has been linked to an increase in gray matter in the brain, which is responsible for executive function, attention, and self-control.

Furthermore, mindfulness and meditation can improve emotional regulation. By becoming more aware of their thoughts and emotions, individuals can learn to recognize and manage difficult emotions such as anger, anxiety, and depression. This can improve overall emotional well-being and reduce the risk of developing mental health disorders.

Additionally, mindfulness and meditation can improve sleep quality. By reducing stress and promoting relaxation, individuals who practice mindfulness or meditation regularly report sleeping better and waking up feeling more rested.

Finally, mindfulness and meditation can lead to a greater sense of well-being and happiness. By developing greater self-awareness, individuals can become more attuned to their needs and values, leading to a more fulfilling and purposeful life.
In conclusion, mindfulness and meditation practices have numerous benefits for individuals' physical, mental, and emotional well-being. From stress reduction to improved focus and concentration, emotional regulation, better sleep, and increased well-being and happiness, the practice of mindfulness and meditation can help individuals live a more fulfilling and healthy life.

In the second book of this series I will provide you with very powerful mindfulness and meditation techniques that aid you from beginner to advanced in creating the ultimate mindset that is in alignment to living your full potential. I've combined 3 systems of wisdom and combined them into one that hasn't been combined before creating a very beneficial system to your progression.

How To Utilize Your Full Potential

4 Fold Breathing and the 4-8 Vagus nerve techniques

Since this is the practical guide I'll start you off with a couple of practical techniques to practicing meditation so that you can get an idea of it and have something to work with to be ready for the next book which will be slightly more complicated but yet again will have beginner to advanced techniques and profoundly more effectiveness .

The 4-fold breathing technique is a simple and effective breathing exercise that is commonly used in meditation to promote relaxation, reduce stress, and increase focus. Here are the steps to perform the technique:

1.Find a comfortable and quiet place to sit, either on a cushion or a chair with a back and straight hands resting on your thighs with your feet flat on the ground, you may also lie down with your hands by your side, legs slightly apart.

2.Take a few deep breaths, inhaling through your nose and exhaling through your mouth. Allow your breath to become slow and steady.

3.Begin by inhaling deeply through your nose for a count of four. Visualize the breath moving from your nose to the bottom of your belly.

4.Hold your breath for a count of four.

5.Exhale slowly through your nose for a count of four. Visualize the breath moving out from the bottom of your belly.

6.Hold your breath out for a count of four.

7.Repeat steps 3 to 6 for several minutes or until you feel relaxed and centered.
As you become more comfortable with the technique, you can increase the length of your inhale, hold, and exhale and hold to a count of six or eight. Try to make each breath even to the next breath where you get an even rhythm going through all the stages of breathing and holding. Remember to focus on your breath and let go of any distracting thoughts by just focusing on the breathwork. This technique can be practiced anytime and anywhere to help you feel calm and centered.

The 4-8 Vagus nerve activation technique

The Vagus nerve is the longest nerve in our body, and it plays a critical role in regulating many bodily functions, including digestion, heart rate, and respiration. The Vagus nerve also plays a key role in the parasympathetic nervous system, which is responsible for the "rest and digest" response.

Activating the Vagus nerve through breathing techniques can help us reduce stress, improve mood, and increase relaxation.

Here's how to perform the Vagus nerve activating breathing technique:

1.Find a comfortable and quiet place to sit or lie down.

2.Breathe deeply and slowly, inhaling through your nose and exhaling through your mouth.

3.Begin to breathe deeply and slowly, inhaling for a count of four and exhaling for a count of eight. This longer exhale will help activate the Vagus nerve.

4.As you exhale, try to focus on your breath and relax your body. Let go of any tension or stress.

5.Continue this breathing pattern for several minutes, focusing on the sensation of your breath and the relaxation in your body.

Remember, taking care of yourself is not selfish or indulgent, but rather a necessary part of achieving your full potential. By prioritizing your physical and mental health, you'll be better equipped to tackle challenges and pursue your goals with confidence and resilience.

Chapter 11
Reviewing And Revising
Your Goals

Setting goals is an important step in achieving your full potential, but it's not enough to just set them and forget about them. It's crucial to regularly review and revise your goals in order to stay on track and make progress towards them.

Here are some tips to help you review and revise your goals effectively:

1.Reflect on your progress:

Take some time to reflect on your progress towards your goals. What have you accomplished so far? What obstacles have you faced? Have you encountered any unexpected challenges or opportunities? Reflecting on your progress can help you gain a better understanding of what's working and what's not, and can help you identify any adjustments that need to be made.

2.Evaluate your goals:

Evaluate the goals you've set for yourself. Are they still relevant and aligned with your values and vision? Are they specific and measurable? Are they realistic and achievable?

How To Utilize Your Full Potential

If any of your goals no longer align with your vision or are unrealistic, it may be time to revise or replace them.

3.Adjust your timeline:

Depending on your progress, you may need to adjust your timeline for achieving your goals. Be realistic and consider any factors that may impact your ability to achieve your goals on the original timeline. Adjusting your timeline can help you avoid feeling overwhelmed or discouraged if you don't make as much progress as you initially anticipated.

4.Break down larger goals:

If you have larger, long-term goals, break them down into smaller, more manageable steps. This can help you stay focused and motivated, and can help you avoid feeling overwhelmed or discouraged. Each small step you take can help you make progress towards your larger goals.

5.Seek feedback:

Consider seeking feedback from a mentor, coach, or trusted friend. They can provide valuable insights and offer suggestions for improvement or adjustment. Sometimes an outside perspective can help you see things in a new light and help you make adjustments that you may not have considered on your own.

6.Stay accountable:

Hold yourself accountable for making progress towards your goals. Keep track of your progress, and regularly assess whether you are staying on track or need to make adjustments. Share your goals and progress with someone else who can help keep you accountable and motivated.

7.Stay kind and generous:

Always help those in need, be it help with anything, words of encouragement, a kind gesture, a thoughtful gift, a friendly shoulder to lean on, someone to talk to. You never know whose life you could be saving by being there for someone. The world is a lonely place for some people, just being there for a minute or two could mean the world to them. Maybe one day they will save you.

8.Stay versatile and flexible:

Remember that things don't always go according to plan. Be flexible and willing to adjust your goals as necessary. If you encounter unexpected obstacles or opportunities, don't be afraid to pivot and adjust your goals accordingly.

9.Stay motivated:

Stay motivated by focusing on the reasons why you set your goals in the first place. Visualize what it will be like to achieve your goals, and remind yourself of the benefits of achieving them. Surround yourself with supportive people who can help keep you motivated and focused.

In summary, reviewing and revising your goals is an ongoing process that is essential for achieving your full potential. By regularly assessing your progress, evaluating your goals, and making necessary adjustments, you can stay on track and make steady progress towards achieving your goals. Remember to stay flexible, seek feedback, and celebrate your successes along the way. With persistence and determination, you can achieve your full potential and live the life you've always dreamed of.

I want to finish this chapter by explaining how important you are in this life with your purpose in mind and your contribution by existing. But all in all the importance is to celebrate this life you live because you only get one chance to enjoy it in the body you dwell in at this moment in time.

Before everything, we are all everlasting energy experiencing a human existence learning from each other. That alone is worth something to celebrate.

The benefits of celebrating your achievements and setting new goals

Celebrating achievements and setting new goals is an important part of personal growth and development. Celebrating one's achievements provides a sense of accomplishment, boosts self-confidence, and motivates individuals to continue striving for success. Setting new goals, on the other hand, provides direction and purpose, helps to maintain focus and motivation, and encourages continued growth and progress.

One of the key benefits of celebrating achievements is improved self-esteem. When individuals celebrate their accomplishments, they acknowledge their hard work and success, which can increase feelings of self-worth and self-confidence. This can lead to greater motivation to continue striving for success in other areas of life.

Celebrating achievements can also provide a sense of closure and completion. When individuals take the time to celebrate their accomplishments, they can reflect on their journey and acknowledge the progress they have made. This can help individuals to move forward with a greater sense of satisfaction and fulfillment.

Moreover, setting new goals provides a sense of direction and purpose. When individuals set new goals, they can focus their energy and efforts on achieving specific outcomes. This can provide a sense of purpose and direction, which can be particularly helpful during times of uncertainty or transition.
Setting new goals also helps individuals to maintain motivation and focus. When

individuals have clear goals in mind, they are more likely to stay focused on their efforts and motivated to work towards their desired outcomes. This can help individuals to overcome obstacles and challenges along the way, leading to greater success.

Finally, setting new goals can lead to continued growth and progress. By setting new goals, individuals challenge themselves to learn new skills and develop new abilities. This can lead to personal and professional growth, as well as improved self-confidence and satisfaction.

In conclusion, celebrating achievements and setting new goals are important aspects of personal growth and development. By celebrating accomplishments, individuals can boost their self-esteem and motivation, while setting new goals provides direction and purpose, maintains focus and motivation, and encourages continued growth and progress.

How To Utilize Your Full Potential

Thank you for reading my first ever published book.

I hope this knowledge can be a reminder of what true self-belief does no matter the circumstances, may it help you in the grand pursuit of achieving your full potential.

I also provide online training and 1-1 coaching for those who seek a more immersive style of learning and less repetition:), within the immediate future, with a subscription, you may have free access to all the future material I will be providing. I'm always on the hunt for the most current cutting edge material combined with universal knowledge, worldly wisdom and resources that aid in the advancements of mental development.

Connect with me @ sumeramindandbodypotentials.durable.co

I'd love to read about your progression and how this book helped you with your greatest endeavors.

Stay tuned-in to my frequency for Book 2 which was a pure joy for me to write and a culmination of spiritual workings, universal knowledge, powerful meditative techniques and practices that continuously helped me overcome, strive and live this life with pure harmony within myself to live to my full potential especially in a time when I was physically bound to a 6ft X 9ft dimensional reality that was heavily limited and in some cases dangerous, but my mind and thoughts were as vast and free as the universe is.

That is a story for yet another book...FS

"You are the greatest project
you will ever get to work on,
it's your time to be alive,
Create Magic
and utilize your
Full Potential "

About The Author

Frank Sumera who was originally born and raised in Vancouver, British Columbia, Canada of Croatian mystical bloodlines is the founder and creator of Sumera Mind and Body Potentials. He has been a resilience/mind-transformational and spiritual life coach for the past 7 years and has lived and worked in multiple countries spanning three separate continents in the past 25+years. He himself has endured a vast multitude of adversity's and gained real life experiences through his travels dealing with different cultural and spiritual influences gaining a wealth of worldly knowledge and wisdom. He spent almost a decade as a practitioner in deep study with over 600+ volumes on spiritual and occult philosophy, psychology, human behavior, self-development and mental transformation.

This is the first part to a 2 part learning series with many more to come connected to Sumera Mind and Body Potentials, his very effective coaching system, that will provide online training programs or live online consultations, or even in person if he is residing or visiting your city otherwise you would have to visit the city he is residing in.

Frank's passion is to help whoever he can that has the desire to fulfill their dreams and goals with his timeless wisdom, experience and practices to reach as far to the stars as they can in acquiring their full potential no matter what age or adversity they are dealing with. Life is too short to waste on suffering, there's a smile to be had at every turning-point. He will inspire you to see that when it comes to life, there are no physical obstacles, just mental blockages that can be broken down to finding the hidden source of talent everyone has always carried within them to gain the life they truly desire. It's just a matter of time before someone comes to their own self-realization.

Frank Sumera welcomes you to connect with him on:
IG @ mindful_evolution888
or sumeramindandbodypotentials.durable.co

Printed in Great Britain
by Amazon

20693485R00054